Quz 144112
B2   5·4
Pts 0·5

WHAT IS LIGHT?

Simon Rose

www.av2books.com

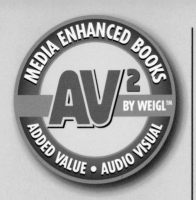

AV² provides enriched content that supplements and complements this bo[ok]. Weigl's AV² books strive to create inspired learning and engage young mi[nds] in a total learning experience.

Your AV² Media Enhanced books come alive with...

Audio
Listen to sections of the book read aloud.

Key Words
Study vocabulary, and complete a matching word activity.

Video
Watch informative video clips.

Quizzes
Test your knowledge.

Embedded Weblinks
Gain additional information for research.

Slide Show
View images and captions, and prepare a presentation.

Try This!
Complete activities and hands-on experiments.

... and much, much mor[e]

Go to www.av2books.com, and enter this book's unique code.

BOOK CODE

D 2 8 3 6 7 5

AV² by Weigl brings you media enhanced books that support active learning.

Published by AV² by Weigl
350 5th Avenue, 59th Floor
New York, NY 10118
Website: www.av2books.com   www.weigl.com

Library of Congress Cataloging-in-Publication Data

Rose, Simon, 1961-
 What is light? / Simon Rose.
   p. cm. -- (Light science)
 Includes index.
 ISBN 978-1-61690-838-6 (hardcover : alk. paper) -- ISBN 978-1-61690-842-3 (softcover : alk. paper) -- ISBN 978-1-61690-388-6 (online)
 1. Light--Juvenile literature. I. Title.
 QC360.R664 2012
 535--dc22

                          2011014130

Printed in the United States of America in North Mankato, Minnesota
1 2 3 4 5 6 7 8 9 0   15 14 13 12 11

052011
WEP290411

Senior Editor: Heather Kissock   Art Director: Terry Paulhus

Weigl acknowledges Getty Images as its primary image supplier for this title.

CONTENTS

Light Notes

Most life on Earth depends on light and the relationship between plants and light. Plants turn sunlight into food through a process called photosynthesis. Photosynthesis is the first step in the **food chain** that connects all living things. Plants are a basic source of food on Earth because all animals eat plants, plant products, or animals that eat other plants.

Studying Light

The world is full of light. The colors of a rainbow, a shadow on the sidewalk, and the pictures on a television screen all come from light. Light is essential to Earth and its residents. Without it, most life on Earth would not be able to survive. Light from the Sun provides **energy** for life on Earth. Without light, Earth would be a dull and lifeless place.

When most people talk about light, they usually mean light that can be seen by humans. However, there are many other kinds of light that humans cannot see. Together, all the different types of light make up the **electromagnetic spectrum**. The tiny part of the electromagnetic spectrum that humans can see is called **visible light**.

Light helps people experience their world. People cannot watch a television show or view content on a computer screen without light being present.

People can only read a book when light shines on its pages.

Light as Energy

Light is a form of energy. This energy is called electromagnetic energy because it is made up of changing electric and **magnetic fields**. The electromagnetic spectrum is comprised of both visible and **invisible** light.

Light is made up of particles of energy called photons. It usually travels as a wave. Visible light is just one part of the waves known as electromagnetic **radiation**. The number of photons indicates how much radiation there is. Fewer photons produce a dim light. A larger number of photons means the light is brighter.

■ When photons hit a surface, they pass their energy off to electrons. The electrons can then be used to create electricity, another form of energy.

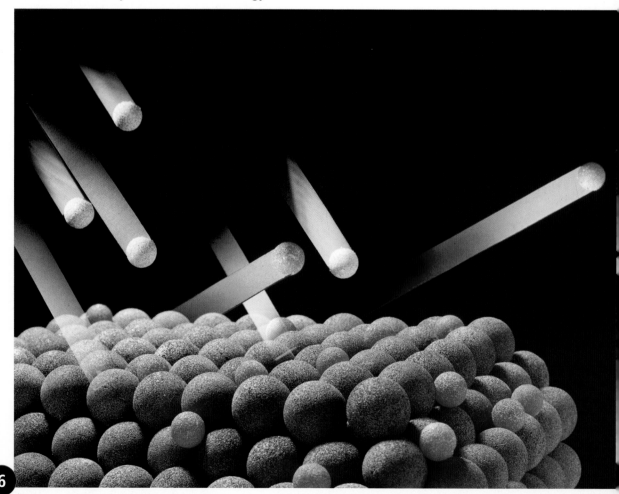

Light is the fastest thing in the universe. In a **vacuum**, light travels at about 186,270 miles (299,792 kilometers) per second. It moves so fast that it can travel around Earth seven times in one second. The Sun is 93 million miles (150 million kilometers) away from Earth. The Sun's light takes about eight minutes to travel to Earth. It would take a particle of light more than 100,000 years to cross the **galaxy** from one side to the other.

■ Besides providing Earth with light, the Sun's energy creates weather by heating the air. Earth would not have wind or rain without the Sun.

Types of Light

Visible light, the small group of light waves in the middle of the electromagnetic spectrum, is the type of light that is most familiar to humans. It is the light that allows people to see objects and colors.

The **wavelengths** located on either side of the visible light spectrum are important as well. These wavelengths are known as invisible light. They are not visible to the human eye.

THE ELECTROMAGNETIC SPECTRUM

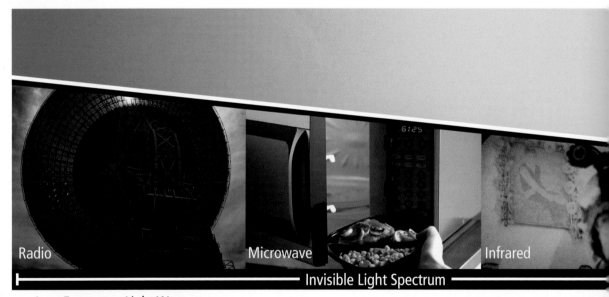

Radio   Microwave   Infrared

Invisible Light Spectrum

Low Frequency Light Wave

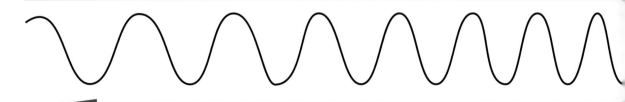

Long Wavelength

Radio waves, microwaves, and infrared radiation are at one end of the electromagnetic spectrum. These types of light have long wavelengths. This means the waves travel slowly. Radio waves are used to send radio and television signals. Microwaves allow people to cook food. Devices using infrared light allow people to see in the dark.

Ultraviolet or UV radiation, X-rays, and gamma rays are at the other end of the spectrum. These types of light have short wavelengths. They are used mostly in medicine. Doctors use X-rays to see if bones are broken. Gamma rays are used to destroy cancer **cells**.

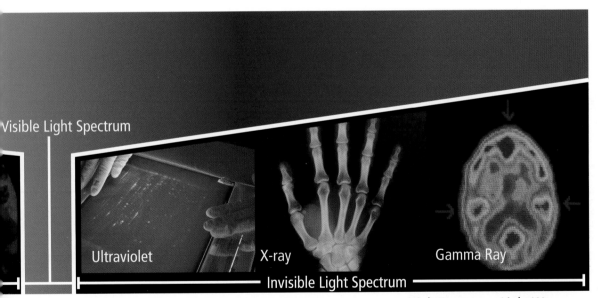

Visible Light Spectrum

Ultraviolet

X-ray

Gamma Ray

Invisible Light Spectrum

High Frequency Light Wave

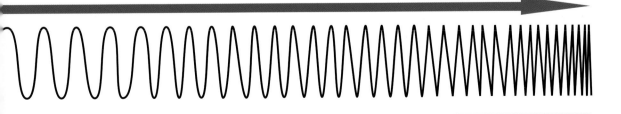

Short Wavelength

The Colors of Visible Light

The visible light spectrum is made up of light from the Sun. This light is called white light. White light is not really white. Instead, it is made up of the colors found in a rainbow—red, orange, yellow, green, blue, indigo, and violet. The colors always appear in this order.

Each of the colors has its own wavelength. These wavelengths are measured in units called nanometers. The length of the waves determines the color of the light. Red has long wavelengths and sits at one end of the spectrum. Violet has short wavelengths and is positioned at the other end.

THE COLORS OF LIGHT

BLACK	RED	ORANGE	YELLOW	GREEN
No light present	Wavelength of 620 to 780 nanometers	Wavelength of 585 to 620 nanometers	Wavelength of 570 to 585 nanometers	Wavelength of 490 to 570 nanometers
No color	A primary color of light			A primary color of light

White light contains the three **primary colors of light**—red, blue, and green. All the other colors are made by mixing these three colors. Light looks white when it contains all three primary colors. When there is no light, there is no color, and black is the result.

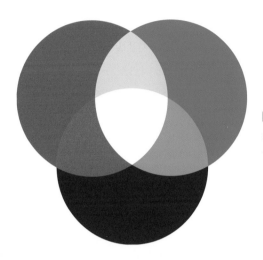

■ Combining red, blue, and green light in different ways can produce all the colors in the visible light spectrum.

BLUE	INDIGO	VIOLET	WHITE
Wavelength of 440 to 490 nanometers	Wavelength of 420 to 440 nanometers	Wavelength of 400 to 420 nanometers	A mixture of all the colors in the visible light spectrum
A primary color of light			

Light and Sight

When light reaches a human eye, a number of steps take place that allow a person to see. Light first enters the human eye through a transparent cover called the cornea. The cornea then bends the light through the eye's lens. The light focuses on the retina, a layer of light-sensitive cells at the back of the eye. These cells are called rods and cones. The rods determine how bright the light is. The cones detect the colors. Once this is done, the retina changes the light into signals. These signals travel through the **optic nerve** to the brain. The brain then reads the signals as an image.

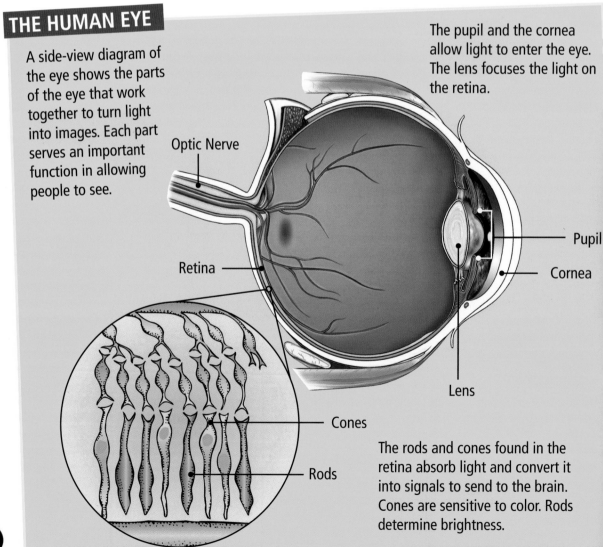

THE HUMAN EYE

A side-view diagram of the eye shows the parts of the eye that work together to turn light into images. Each part serves an important function in allowing people to see.

The pupil and the cornea allow light to enter the eye. The lens focuses the light on the retina.

Optic Nerve

Retina

Pupil

Cornea

Lens

Cones

Rods

The rods and cones found in the retina absorb light and convert it into signals to send to the brain. Cones are sensitive to color. Rods determine brightness.

In order to see clearly, the amount of light coming from an object must be regulated. In near-darkness, the pupil—the dark spot in the center of the human eye—expands, or gets bigger. This allows more light into the eye. In bright sunlight, the pupil contracts, or gets smaller. This protects the eye from being flooded with light. This process takes a moment or two. This is why it takes a few seconds for a person's eyes to adjust to light and dark.

COLOR BLINDNESS

Some humans are color blind. This means that they cannot perceive as many colors as people with normal vision. Most people who are color blind have trouble seeing reds and greens. About eight percent of males have some form of color blindness. Only 0.4 percent of females are affected by color blindness.

To test for color blindness, doctors show patients pictures made up of different colored dots. A person who is color blind will not be able to see the pattern within the dots.

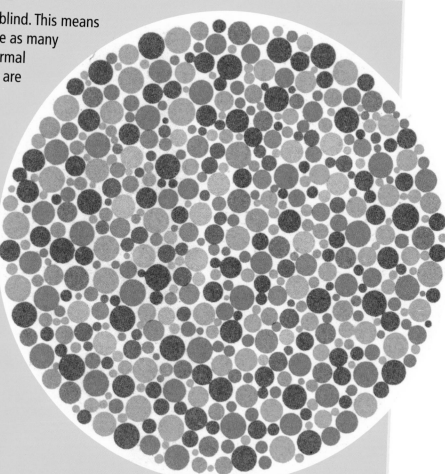

Making Color

Every time a person sees a colored object, some of the light is **reflected**, and some is **absorbed**. The wavelength that is reflected to the eye gives the object its color. The rest of the wavelengths are absorbed into the object. Therefore, an apple appears red because it reflects red light and a banana seems yellow because it reflects yellow light.

If the color of an object is black, it means that no light has been reflected from that object and that all the light waves have been absorbed. White objects, on the other hand, appear white because they reflect all light waves.

■ A plant's leaves absorb all of the colors in the color spectrum except green. Green is reflected. This is why the leaves appear green to the human eye.

Light Discoveries Through Time

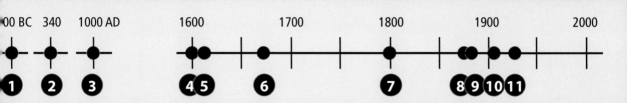

00 BC   340   1000 AD   1600   1700   1800   1900   2000

1   **2**   **3**   **4 5**   **6**   **7**   **8 9 10 11**

1 **400 BC**
Plato proposes that light rays come from the eyes and help people see.

2 **340 BC**
Aristotle states that light is a **static** force that does not move.

3 **Around 1000 AD**
Alhazen suggests that light travels between objects and the eye.

4 **1600s**
Galileo attempts to measure the speed of light.

5 **1604**
Johannes Kepler discovers that light rays reach the retina, where they are processed and sent to the brain.

6 **1672**
Isaac Newton determines that white light is made up of several colors.

7 **1800**
Sir Frederick William Herschel discovers infrared light. He is the first person to discover that there are forms of light that people cannot see.

8 **1873**
James Clerk Maxwell determines that light is electromagnetic energy.

9 **1879**
Thomas Edison develops the first long-lasting light bulb.

10 **1905**
Albert Einstein suggests that light consists of particles called photons.

11 **1927**
Scientists agree that light functions using both particles and waves.

The position of a light source will affect the size and shape of an object's shadow.

Shadow Play

Shadows occur when something blocks light from its source. If light hits a solid object before it arrives at another solid object, a shadow is formed. The shadow shows the outline of the object that is blocking the light.

There are some objects that people can see through and some they cannot. A transparent object is one that allows most of the light it comes in contact with to pass through it. A translucent object allows some light to pass through. An opaque object does not allow any light through. Many solid objects, including wood, stone, and metal, are opaque to visible light. These objects will cast a shadow.

The size of the shadow gets smaller as the object is moved away from the light source. For example, if a ball is near a light bulb, it casts a large shadow on the wall. If the ball is placed farther away from the light bulb, it blocks less light, so the shadow is smaller.

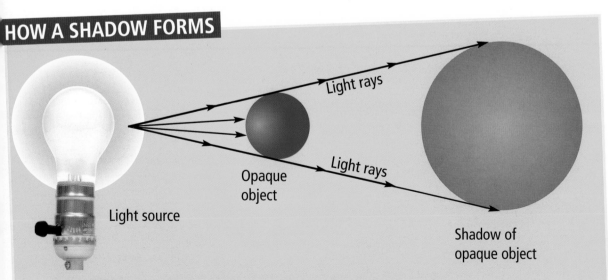

HOW A SHADOW FORMS

Light rays

Light rays

Opaque object

Light source

Shadow of opaque object

When light hits an opaque object, the object blocks the movement of the light. The light can travel on either side of the object but cannot reach behind it. A shadow showing the outline of the object appears instead.

Shadows in Space

At certain times, Earth and its Moon form a line with the Sun in their **orbits**. This causes what is known as an eclipse. An eclipse is a shadow in space.

A lunar eclipse happens when the Moon orbits into Earth's shadow. Earth blocks some of the Sun's light, preventing it from reaching the Moon. A total lunar eclipse occurs when Earth's shadow completely covers the Moon. During a partial eclipse, the Moon is only partly covered by Earth's shadow.

A solar eclipse occurs when the Moon moves between the Sun and Earth. The Moon blocks part of the Sun's light, and the Moon's shadow is cast onto the surface of the Earth. When there is a new moon and the Sun and Moon are in a perfect line, it is called a total eclipse. During a partial eclipse, only part of the Sun and Moon overlap.

■ Earth experiences two to five solar eclipses each year.

What is an Optics Physicist?

The study of light is known as optics. Optics is part of a science called **physics**. Physicists who study optics are interested in the behavior and **properties** of light. They observe how light interacts with objects and other matter. Some optics physicists develop instruments that help them learn more about how light works.

Optics physicists enjoy experimenting with light. They must be able to think creatively but still use scientific theories. They have an aptitude for mathematics and physics. Most are fascinated with the way the physical world works in relation to the speed of light and optical technology.

James Clerk Maxwell

James Clerk Maxwell was a Scottish physicist. While researching **theories** on magnetism and electricity in the late 1800s, Maxwell discovered that light was an electromagnetic wave. This research has led to much of the technology in the world today, including radio, television, and satellite communication.

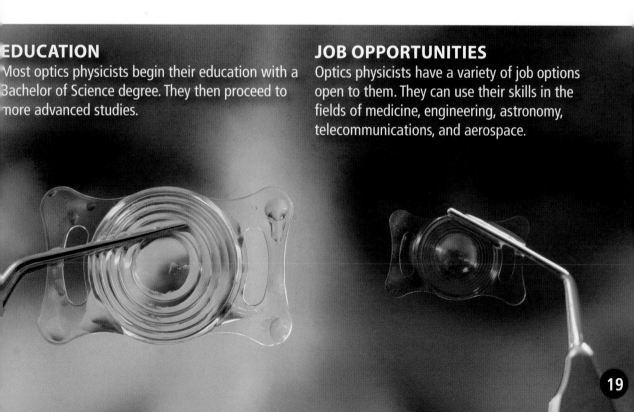

EDUCATION
Most optics physicists begin their education with a Bachelor of Science degree. They then proceed to more advanced studies.

JOB OPPORTUNITIES
Optics physicists have a variety of job options open to them. They can use their skills in the fields of medicine, engineering, astronomy, telecommunications, and aerospace.

Seven Facts About Light

Up to 80 percent of the Sun's rays can filter through cloud, fog, and mist.

The human eye can process 36,000 pieces of information every hour.

Although nothing can move faster than light, light was stopped in its tracks in 2001. Scientists can now stop light, store it, and release it whenever they want.

Harmful ultraviolet rays damage the skin. Apply a large amount of sunscreen 15 to 30 minutes before going outdoors.

Light comes from two main sources—natural and human made.

The Moon is not a source of light. It merely reflects light from the Sun.

Some plants and animals glow. This ability is called bioluminescence.

Light Brain Teasers

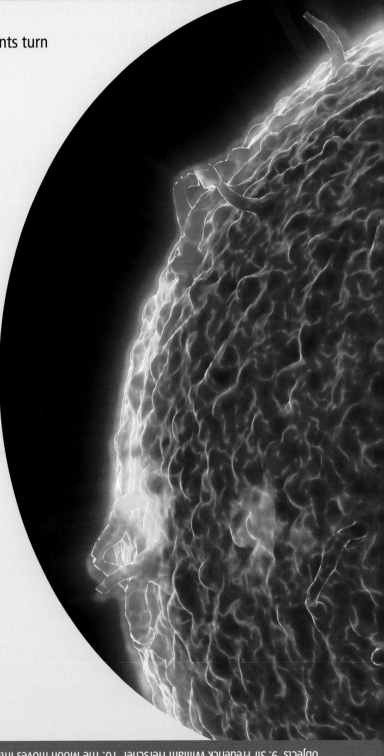

1 What is the process by which plants turn sunlight into food?

2 What is the electromagnetic spectrum?

3 How does light normally travel?

4 What type of light can be used to show objects in the dark?

5 What are rods and cones?

6 What are the three primary colors of light?

7 What determines the color of an object?

8 Which types of objects cast shadows?

9 Who was the first person to discover invisible light?

10 What happens during a lunar eclipse?

ANSWERS: 1. Photosynthesis 2. All forms of light, both visible and invisible 3. As a wave 4. Infrared light 5. Light-sensitive cells that detect color and brightness 6. Red, blue, and green 7. Reflected light 8. Opaque objects 9. Sir Frederick William Herschel 10. The Moon moves into Earth's shadow

Science in Action

Casting Shadows

Test your knowledge of casting shadows with this experiment. Remember that the length of an object's shadow depends on the location of the light source in relation to the object.

Tools Needed

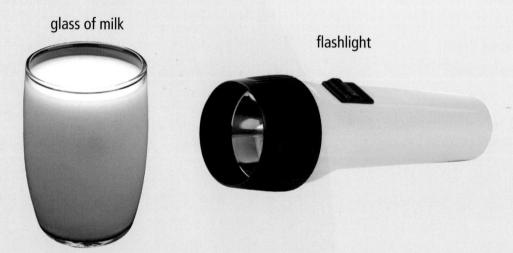

glass of milk

flashlight

Directions

1 Place the glass of milk on a table.

2 Turn the flashlight on, and move it to different positions in front of the glass of milk. Observe the length of the shadow behind the glass of milk.

3 Where is the flashlight when you make
a) the longest shadow?
b) the shortest shadow?
c) the widest shadow?
d) the narrowest shadow?

Words to Know

absorbed: taken in and held without reflecting back

cells: the very small, basic units of living matter

electromagnetic spectrum: the entire range of wavelengths of light energy, from radio to gamma, including visible light

energy: the capacity for doing work

food chain: a group of living things that form a chain to show how energy is passed from one living thing to another

galaxy: a very large group of stars

invisible: not able to be seen by the human eye

magnetic fields: the space around a magnet in which the magnet has the power to attract other metals

optic nerve: the nerve that sends messages about light and color from the eyes to the brain

orbits: paths that space objects follow as they circle around another object

physics: the science of matter and energy and their interactions

primary colors of light: the three colors of light from which all colors can be obtained through mixing

properties: characteristics that are unique to a certain object

radiation: energy given off in the form of waves or tiny particles

reflected: turned or thrown back

static: showing little or no growth, change, or movement

theories: a group of principles that explain why or how something happens

vacuum: a space that is completely empty of matter

visible light: the part of the electromagnetic spectrum that can be detected by the human eye

wavelengths: the distance between the top of one wave to the top of the one directly after it

Index

Log on to www.av2books.com

AV² by Weigl brings you media enhanced books that support active learning. Go to www.av2books.com, and enter the special code found on page 2 of this book. You will gain access to enriched and enhanced content that supplements and complements this book. Content includes video, audio, web links, quizzes, a slide show, and activities.

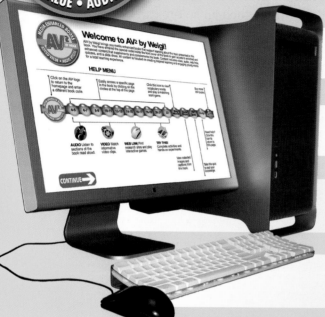

Audio
Listen to sections of the book read aloud.

Video
Watch informative video clips.

Embedded Weblinks
Gain additional information for research.

Try This!
Complete activities and hands-on experiments.

WHAT'S ONLINE?

Try This!	Embedded Weblinks	Video	EXTRA FEATURES
Complete an activity to learn more about light.

Learn more about the history of light research with a timeline activity.

Write about a day in the life of a researcher who works with light.

Test your knowledge of light with a fact activity. | Learn more about light.

Find out more about how light reveals the world.

Learn more about the science of light. | Watch this video to learn more about light.

Watch a video about a technology that uses light. | |

Audio
Listen to sections of the book read aloud.

Key Words
Study vocabulary, and complete a matching word activity.

Slide Show
View images and captions and prepare a presentation

Quizzes
Test your knowledge.

AV² was built to bridge the gap between print and digital. We encourage you to tell us what you like and what you want to see in the future.

Sign up to be an AV² Ambassador at www.av2books.com/ambassador.